Anxiety Relief Activity Book

Draw, Paint, Color, Doodle, and Write Your Way to Calm

Leah Guzman, ATR-BC

CALLISTO PUBLISHING

Copyright © 2023 by Callisto Publishing LLC
Cover and internal design © 2023 by Callisto Publishing LLC
Illustrations by Paperface with the following exceptions: Shutterstock: © chempina: cover (brush);
© Lermot: cover (pencil & scissors), v (scissors), back cover (pencil); © Strawberry Blossom: 3, back
cover left; © milezaway: 19; © Tapkimonkey: 31; © le adhiz: 39, 79; © OlichO: 43, 83; © Curly Pat:
59, 71 iStock/Getty Images: © Miriam2009: 11; © 94clover: 23, back cover right; © Katsiaryna
Hedroich: 51; © saemilee: 63; © Veeraphong: 91

Art Director: Brieanna Felschow
Art Producer: Stacey Stambaugh
Editor: Mo Mozuch
Production Editor: Rachel Taenzler
Production Manager: Riley Hoffman

Published by Callisto Publishing LLC C/O Sourcebooks LLC
P.O. Box 4410, Naperville, Illinois 60567-4410
(630) 961-3900
callistopublishing.com

Printed and bound in China.
1010 10 9 8 7 6 5 4 3 2 1

**DEDICATED
TO MY PARENTS:**

My dad, who enlightened
me to cherish the little
moments in life, and my
mom, who taught me
resilience.

INTRODUCTION

Are you suffering from anxiety? Are you looking for ways to help you manage and understand your anxiety? Then this book is for you. My name is Leah Guzman, and I am a practicing artist and art therapist with more than twenty years of experience helping people with anxiety. I hold a board certification in art therapy and use it to provide my patients with the skills they need to cope with anxiety.

Anxiety is a common reaction to stress and may be triggered by a variety of situations. Even though everyone can experience anxiety, each person's situation is unique. I suffered from extreme panic attacks until I got support from a trained art therapist who helped me address and resolve my issues. If you are suffering from anxiety to the point that it's interfering with your daily functioning, you may want to consider consulting a trained professional. Even though I'm a board-certified art therapist, this book is not "therapy" in the traditional sense. This book is meant to help you relax, provide a creative outlet, and distract you from your anxious thoughts. Engaging in the activities within this book will help you focus on something fun, provide peace in your life, and allow you to be expressive.

HOW TO USE THIS BOOK

This book is filled with fun! It has detailed instructions designed to help you create amazing artwork. Activities include drawing, painting, collage-making, journaling, and more. The drawing prompts ask you to playfully interact with the page by adding your own symbols, colors, and imagery. In the painting prompts, you will be expressing your feelings through color. Collage-making involves cutting out pictures and combining them with different colors and shapes to create an image. The act of flipping through magazines and clipping the elements of your collage is repetitive and relaxing. The journal prompts are designed to connect you with your anxious thoughts in a useful way. Reverse coloring pages may look like finished watercolor paintings, but these spaces are for you to add your own lines and doodles to create dynamic designs. Along with traditional coloring pages, these mindfulness exercises are extremely satisfying.

Below is a list of materials you can use in this book. Avoid using watercolor paint, because it will cause the paper to warp, and don't use nail polish, because it will cause pages to stick together. Go ahead and gather your supplies. Consider placing them in a tote, along with this book, to use throughout your day.

- ✦ Acrylic paint
- ✦ Brushes
- ✦ Colored pencils
- ✦ Glue stick

- ✦ Magazines and construction paper for collage
- ✦ Markers
- ✦ Pens
- ✦ Scissors

Have fun with the activities and use this book however it serves you best to relax, create, and bring yourself happiness.

Release what isn't for you so you can receive what you want. On the left hand, draw what you are releasing because it is no longer serving you (e.g., fear, doubt, shame, procrastination). On the right hand, draw what you wish to call in (e.g., love, community, self-care, creativity, patience).

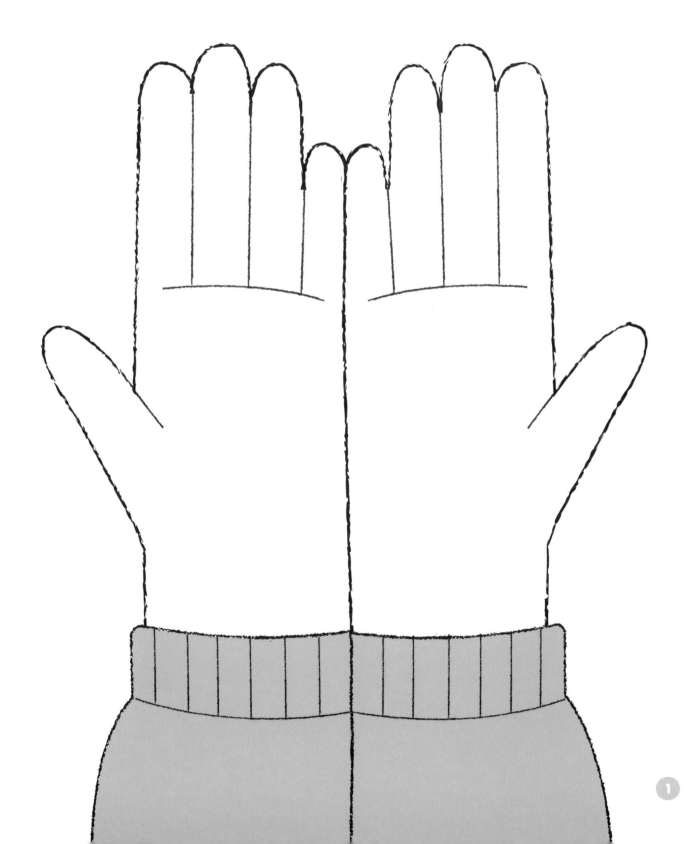

Dot grid pattern play is a focused activity that can bring you into a meditative state. In this exercise, you will continue the pattern that has been started for you. Follow the lines and connect the dots, then continue the pattern by making concentric circles. When you finish, color in the design.

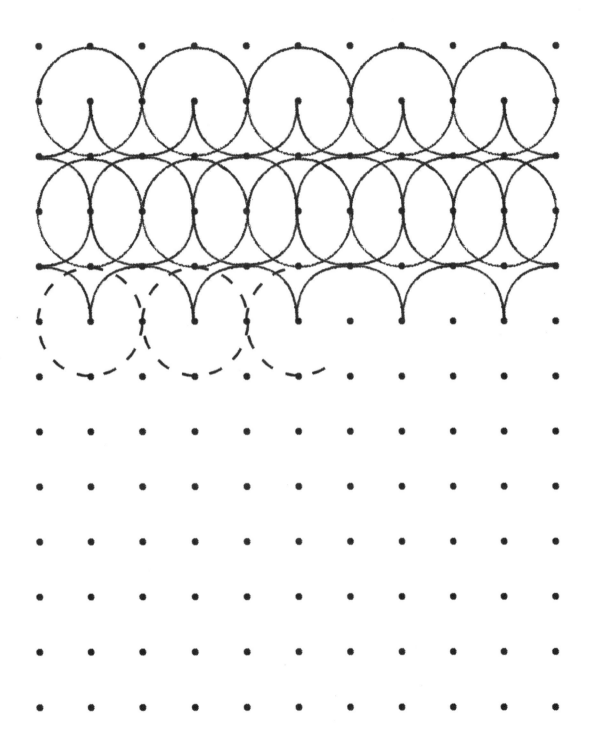

One simple tool to calm worried thoughts is to scan the space you are in. Name several objects that are important to you (e.g., coffee, phone, window). Write about how grateful you are for each object and what it does for you. Be as silly or as serious as you want!

_____

_____

_____

_____

_____

_____

_____

_____

_____

_____

_____

_____

_____

_____

_____

_____

_____

_____

_____

_____

_____

_____

_____

_____

Breathing techniques can help calm your mind. Give it a try by dipping a paintbrush into your favorite color. Connect with your breath while you do. Take a deep breath in as you paint a figure eight like the one shown. As you exhale, move the paint into another figure eight. Continue making figure eights, as necessary, to relax your body.

Repeat the calming mantra "Peace begins with me" as you clip out small squares from magazines, cloth, or assorted papers. Organize the clipped squares by color and then glue the pieces to the page to fill in the peace sign.

PEACE BEGINS WITH ME

Write a brief letter to your inner artist, as if you were writing to a loved one. What do you want to say to your creative side? What words would inspire and make this relationship come alive? Are you craving art time? Make a date.

The mind is like a garden. When watered and nurtured, it will grow. On the brain side, write some of your anxious thoughts. Then write your favorite positive affirmations in the blooms below, and decorate them with uplifting and inspiring colors.

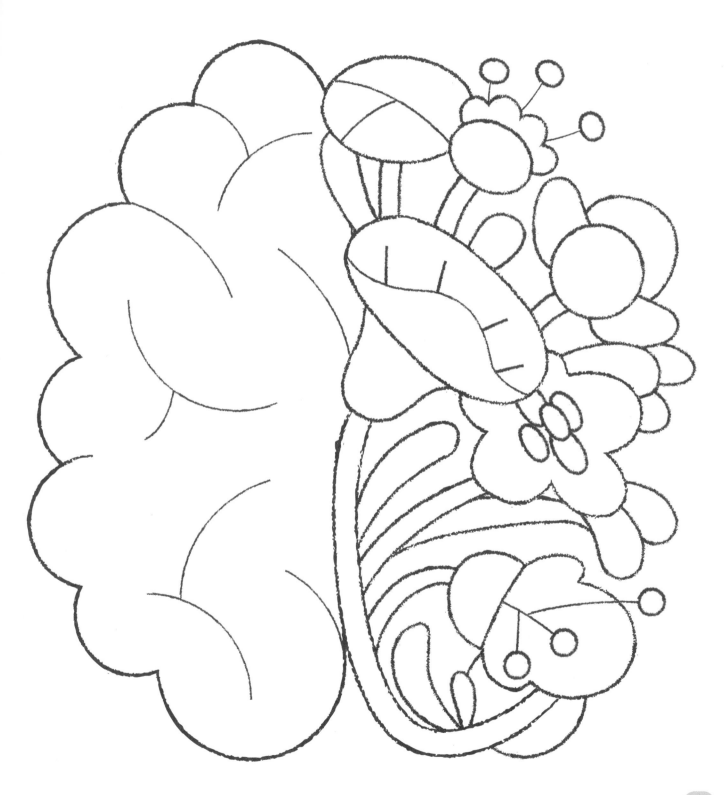

Make a silly face that represents your anxiety and take a picture of yourself. The photograph can be of your face or entire body. Print the image on a sheet of paper. Cut the image of yourself out and glue it in the space provided. Add paint, lines, and symbols that represent the anxiety you feel.

Make a self-care collage. What are some of your daily or weekly routines that make you feel good? For example, using this book is one way to take care of yourself! Pick out some fun images from magazines, or print ones you find online, that feature activities that nurture your soul and glue them here in any arrangement you like.

Imagine that a package arrives in the mail for you. To your surprise, you were gifted a beautiful golden magic lamp. You playfully rub the lamp, and a genie bursts out. You are granted the opportunity to make three wishes. What would you ask for?

1. _____
_____
_____
_____
_____
_____

2. _____
_____
_____
_____
_____
_____
_____
_____

3. _____
_____
_____
_____
_____
_____
_____

We all have different parts to our personalities. A part of our personality that we don't like is called our shadow. The shadow may show up as anxiety or frustration. What's in your shadow? What aspects of yourself do you like? Draw images and symbols for both sides.

Use your available senses to choose a soothing element from your surroundings. In the figure provided, draw symbols representing the senses on the fingers. When you feel anxious, bring yourself back to this image and let it serve as a reminder to help you choose a soothing element from around you.

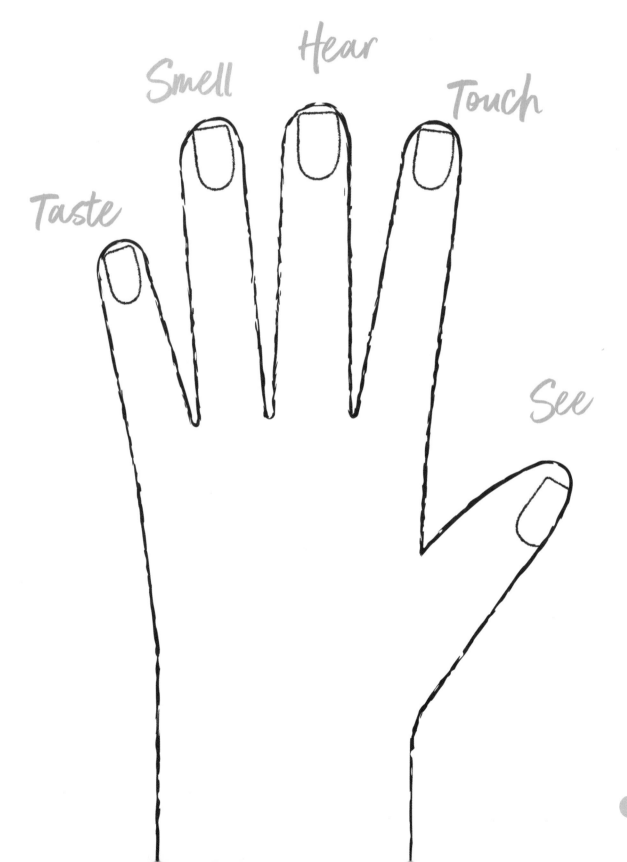

Use the space provided for a brain dump of all your pressing thoughts. It can be a to-do list, some important decisions, or anything else that's weighing on your mind. When you're done, circle what you consider to be the three most important items right now. Give them your attention today.

Anxiety is often associated with fire imagery. It can be kindled by different uncomfortable emotions and, in turn, intensify them. In the figure provided, paint the flames with colors that represent the types of discomfort you experience from anxiety. You can add additional feelings and emotions to the flames if you need to.

Spark your creativity by flipping through magazines and cutting out images that resonate with how you want to feel. Find images that bring a sense of calm. Pick colors and phrases that make you feel uplifted. The act of cutting paper itself can be a soothing, repetitive exercise, but you can also glue your collection in the space provided.

Paint the rainbow of uplifting thoughts. Sometimes we can be hard on ourselves, and negative self-talk can take over our mind. When that happens, it is important to change what we say to ourselves and show ourselves some self-compassion. Self-compassion is a self-care practice. As you paint each hue in the rainbow, say the affirmation out loud!

Anxiety arises in moments when we are worried about the future.
Complete the sentences.

1. I felt anxious when _____
    _____
    _____.

2. I had hoped for _____
    _____
    _____.

3. I know that _____
    _____
    _____.

4. I'm ready for _____
    _____
    _____.

5. I understand _____
    _____
    _____.

6. I trust _____
    _____
    _____.

7. I'm ready to feel _____
    _____
    _____.

Grounding exercises are an effective way to calm your nervous system. You do this by using your available senses. In this activity, you will be painting the grounding rocks your favorite colors. Some of the rocks are labeled with a grounding experience for you to try, and the others are blank so you can create your own.

It's fun to visualize places that wash away worries. Close your eyes. Take a moment to visualize yourself at the beach. Imagine the rolling waves taking away your stress. Use the space provided to draw yourself in the beach scene. Add items you would bring with you.

How is anxiety showing up for you emotionally, physically, and in your actions?
Fill in the table below with:

- ✦ Three emotions that come up for you when you are anxious about a specific situation
- ✦ Three physical symptoms you feel in your body
- ✦ Three actions you can take right now

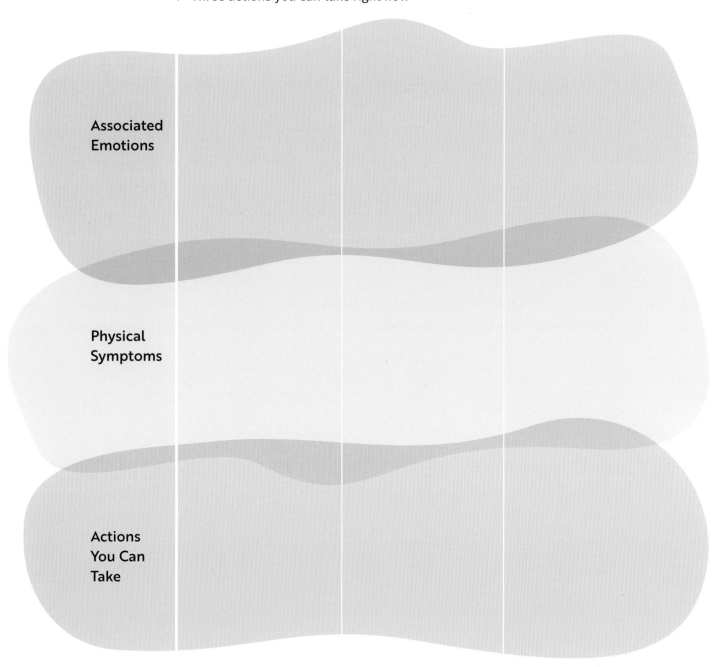

Associated Emotions

Physical Symptoms

Actions You Can Take

Anxiety can be high one day and low another day. Go ahead and rate your anxiety, with a 10 being extreme (having a panic attack) and 1 representing feeling calm. Consider coloring one of the provided thermometers whenever you feel anxious as a way to gauge the intensity of your anxiety. This is a great way to check in.

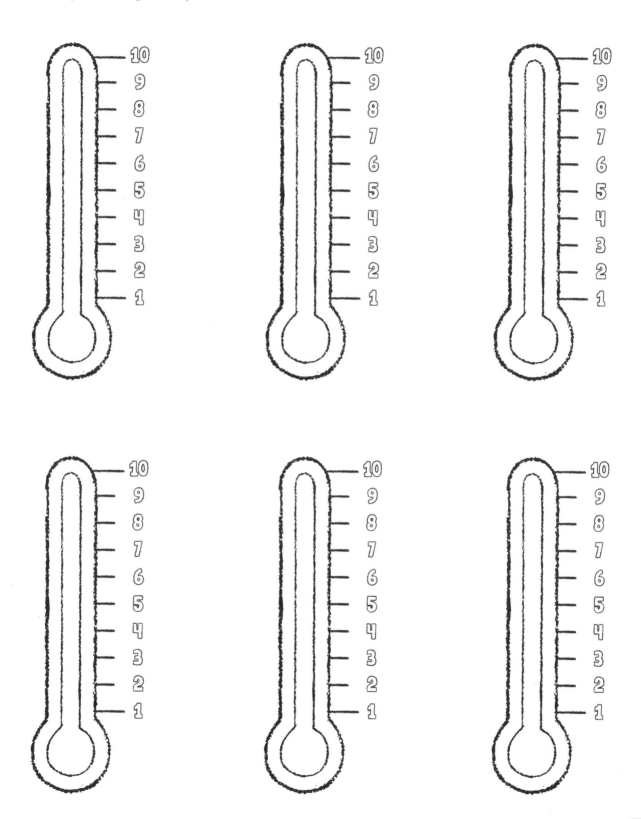

There are always two sides of every situation. Many times, we think the worst may happen, which leads to anxiety. In the space provided, draw out the worst-case scenario on one side of the page. On the other side of the page, draw what you see as the best-case scenario for the situation.

WORST

BEST

Draw your anxiety as a monster! Think about all the details of the monster. What is its facial expression? What color is its skin? What would it be wearing? Would it be big or small? What is your monster doing?

Now is your opportunity to speak to your anxiety monster. What do you want to say to it? Think about when the anxiety monster shows up for you in your day. If you could have a relationship with the monster, what words would you say to get to know it better?

The story of Pandora's box—a sealed box containing all human misery—originated in Greek mythology. In this activity, you can put your troubles and misery into the box! Inside the box provided, draw symbols of situations that cause you anxiety that you would like to seal in a box and store away.

Think about a special place you would like to visit. Cut images from magazines or brochures, or print out imagery of the place and glue it in the space provided. Add activities that you would like to experience while you are there. In the remaining space, include how you believe it would feel for you to experience the trip.

What are your current thoughts that trigger your worry? Go ahead and make a list of current worries on one side of the page. Take a moment to stretch your imagination and envision the best-case scenario for each situation. Pick one and draft your amazing new story.

WORRIES	BEST CASE

MY NEW STORY

Labyrinths are designed to foster contemplation and transformation. Use your paintbrush and favorite colors to follow the path into the center and then follow the path back out again. You can add layers of colors to your labyrinth to find inner peace.

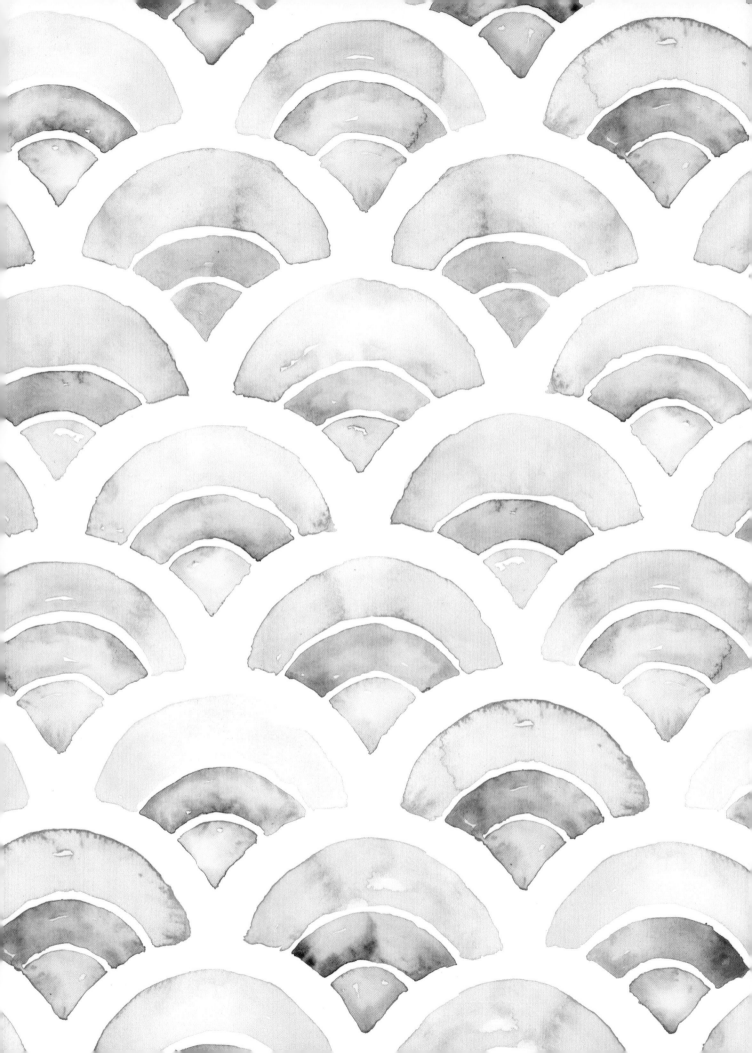

Body scans help you pinpoint where in your body you hold your anxiety. Where do you hold anxiety? Is it in your head, shoulders, belly, or another place? Is it in a combination of places? In the figure provided, use paint to color the areas where you are holding your anxiety. Choose colors that best represent the nature of your anxiety.

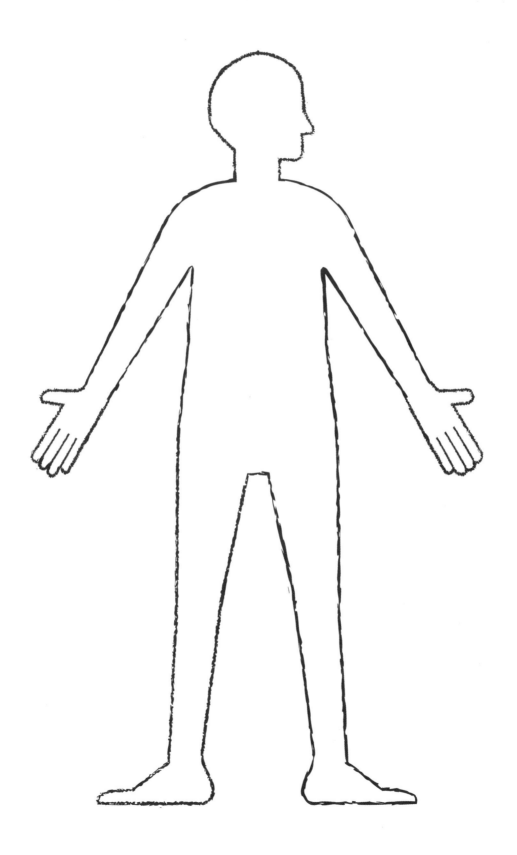

Look at the imagery provided and choose two ideas that resonate with you. Imagine a story happening between the two ideas you chose. Draw the story with those images and add additional imagery, as necessary, to create your story. Use your imagination and get creative.

Using the visual imagery you created in the last exercise as a basis, write your story in the space provided. Give it a title. When you are done writing your story, think about what feelings are associated with the drawing. What might happen after the events in the story?

The image of a winding path represents life's journey. Focus on one square at a time as you fill in the lines to re-create the image of a winding path. Once you have sketched out the design, you can add colors to bring the imagery to life.

Anxiety can feel like extra energy. Go ahead and play your favorite song. Engage in some healthy movement while listening to it to shake off the extra energy, then use this space to draw the lines, symbols, and other elements that represent your chosen song.

Word associations are a fun way to list ideas. Fill in the numbered blanks with the first words that pop into your mind related to the word listed. Give three examples for each one. Consider thinking of other feelings or situations and repeating the activity.

UNCOMFORTABLE

① _____

② _____

③ _____

FEAR

① _____

② _____

③ _____

NERVOUSNESS

① _____

② _____

③ _____

EXCITEMENT

① _____

② _____

③ _____

COZY

① _____

② _____

③ _____

PEACE

① _____

② _____

③ _____

Look around your room and choose an object to represent you. Draw the object's outline. Now, fill the drawing with shapes and lines representing your anxiety level. Illustrate your anxiety by creating bubbles, jagged lines, and swirls. When complete, the assembled figure visually represents your level of anxiety.